Walking with Our Ancestors

Walking with Our Ancestors

Contemplation and Activism

BARBARA A. HOLMES

FORTRESS PRESS
MINNEAPOLIS

WALKING WITH OUR ANCESTORS
Contemplation and Activism

Library of Congress Cataloging-in-Publication Data

Names: Holmes, Barbara Ann, author.
Title: Walking with our ancestors : contemplation and activism / Barbara A. Holmes.
Description: Minneapolis : Fortress Press, [2023] | Includes bibliographical references.
Identifiers: LCCN 2023029087 (print) | LCCN 2023029088 (ebook) | ISBN 9781506499239 (print) | ISBN 9781506499246 (ebook)
Subjects: LCSH: African Americans--Civil rights. | Civil rights--United States--Religious aspects--Christianity. | Civil rights movements--United States. | Contemplation. | African American civil rights workers. | United States--Race relations.
Classification: LCC E185.615 .H59 2023 (print) | LCC E185.615 (ebook) | DDC 323.1196/073--dc23/eng/20230810
LC record available at https://lccn.loc.gov/2023029087
LC ebook record available at https://lccn.loc.gov/2023029088

Cover image: Digital collage with Colors of Humanity Series - stock illustration by marthadavies/Getty Images
Cover design: Kristin Miller

Print ISBN: 978-1-5064-9923-9
eBook ISBN: 978-1-5064-9924-6

Contents

CONTENTS

Ain't Gonna Let Nobody Turn Us Around

Each generation leaves a legacy to succeeding generations. . . . That legacy may be solid, etched in stone, or it may be as fragile as a house of cards, tumbling in the first gust of wind.

—Barbara Jordan

At the heart of the universe is a higher reality— God and [God's] kingdom of love—to which we must all be conformed.

—Martin Luther King Jr.

The authentic mystic can never flee the world. He or she must resonate with the suffering and agony that is the common legacy of humankind . . . and active mystics who live in the hurly-burly enter into the same inner silence as those who live in the desert.

—William Johnston

> In Afro-American spirituality there is no contra-
> diction between contemplation and social action.
> There is no contempt for the world, but contempt
> for the world as it presently is.
>
> —James A. Noel

The world is the cloister of the contemplative. There is no escape. Always the quest for justice draws one deeply into the heart of God. In this sacred interiority, contemplation becomes the language of prayer and the impetus for prophetic proclamation and action. Martin Luther King Jr. and Rosa Parks were classic contemplatives, deeply committed to silent witness, embodied and performative justice. The type of contemplative practices that emerged during the civil rights movement became dramas that enacted a deep discontentment with things as they were. For years, the Black Church nurtured its members in the truth of their humanity and the potential for moral flourishing. Worship practices and songs like "You Got a Right" ritualized liberation and reminded denigrated people of God's promises.

As with all great social justice movements, there came a time when worship practices and communal resolve coalesced, and an interfaith, interdenominational, interracial community formed. The commonality for this dissenting community was the willingness to resist the power of apartheid in the Americas with their bodies. This intercultural resistance coalition had to overcome not just the external evil but also the evil that had been internalized. Among people of color, issues included anger, self-hatred, and oppression-induced lethargy; among members of the dominant culture, the lust for power and an ethos of control and imperialism skewed relational possibilities.

And yet a community committed to justice formed. It was in many respects similar to the *communitas* gathering that Victor Turner's research revealed.[1] A community is not always an intentional gathering of like-minded people who munch on coffee and donuts as they assess issues of common concern. Sometimes communities form because unpredictable events and circumstances draw people into shared life intersections. Those trapped on planes and in towers on 9/11 became instantaneous communities as they faced death and struggled with cell-phone good-byes. Their individuality is not lost as we remember them, but their identity is contextually grounded in a shared life experience that I would call community. Communities form when ego focused concerns recede in favor of shared agendas and a more universal identity. These relationships need only hold together briefly before transitioning into other forms; however, while they are intact, all concerned are aware of the linkages of interior resolve that are at work.

Identifying the Power Source

Most attribute the power of the civil rights movement to the institutional Black Church. This is only true in part. Clearly, the Black Church was the womb that nurtured the hope of that social eventuality, but the spark that ignited the justice movements did not come from the hierarchical institutional Black Church. Rather, it was the quixotic and limber heart of that institution, its flexible, spiritually open, and mystical center, that ignited first the young people and then their elders to move their symbolic initiatives from ritual ring shouts to processional and contemplative marches.

The formation of community during the civil rights movement was the quintessential coming-of-age story for Africana people. During a particular time in history, nonviolent initiatives seeded with contemplative worship practices became acts of public theology and activism. Activism and contemplation are not functional opposites. Rather, contemplation is, at its heart, a reflective activity that is always seeking the spiritual balance between individual piety and communal justice seeking. I am suggesting that the genesis of the great justice movements of the twentieth century emerged from the consistent contemplative practices of those seeking liberation. This premise is supported by history, from the passive resistance of Mohandas Gandhi, Rosa Parks, and Martin Luther King Jr. to the social protests of Daniel Berrigan, Fannie Lou Hamer, Malcolm X (El Hajj Malik El Shabazz), Nelson Mandela, and Black Lives Matter protesters. Each social stance is linked to the stalwart interiority of visionary individuals and their co-laboring communities.

Since the civil rights movement wound down and equal opportunity for all became the prevailing social presumption, the Africana community in North America has been hurtling toward potential destruction and transformation. I suggest these two socio-spiritual destinations not as polarities but as a motley mix of undifferentiated options that tug the community "every which way but loose." Every gain is seeded with just enough destruction, personal and communal, to deflate and nullify the overall sense of accomplishment. Each failure carries upon its horizon the hope and "overcoming" determination of the ancestors that cannot be denied even in the midst of abandonment of social goals in favor of consumerism, crime, and the skewing of moral values.

To be certain, the desire to prove self-worth and wipe out a history of oppression in one generation has taken its spiritual toll. Something is needed in the spiritual lives of Africana people. I am proposing that this "something" must include a healing reclamation of a unique Africana contemplative heritage, its communal rituals and practices both silent and oral.

Even in its most passive aspects, contemplation plugs the supplicants into the catalytic center of God's Spirit, into the divine power that permeates every aspect of life. In this space, there are no false dichotomies, no divisions between the sacred and the secular. James Noel makes the connection between Black spirituality and social action very plain: "any spirituality which does not engage in justice is unbiblical and only reinforces the political and psychic structures of oppression."[1] Noel infers that the very essence of Christianity is its moral plumb line, its mandate to "do justice." Through acts of contemplation, individuals and congregations enter the liminal space where the impossible becomes possible. The liminal vantage point described by Victor Turner offers the ability to "see clearly," to critique the prisms of oppression reflected even in the victims. Those privy to this perspective can "reconfigure the status quo with hope, and then . . . implement hope with social action."[2]

From a Christian perspective, the quest for justice begins with participation in the claim that we are redeemed by a suffering Savior. In theological circles, the suffering that precedes redemption is interpreted as an emotionally distant but efficacious moral example, as a meaningful liturgical moment worthy of reenactment, as an ancient historical reality, or, in the case of many Africana congregations, as a present and accessible portal to the current and immediate suffering of the community. This immediacy lends itself to personal and communal transformation through the mystery of spiritual union.

In the words of Simone Weil, the person whose "soul remains orientated towards God while a nail is driven through it finds himself nailed to the very center of the universe; the true center, which is not in the middle, which is not in space and time, which is God." Weil goes on to say that "without leaving the time and place to which the body is bound, the soul can traverse the whole of space and time and come into the actual presence of God."[3] It is in this presence that the path forward becomes clearer and the implementation of spiritual energy is directed.

The activism that ignited the freedom movements had contemplative practices at its center. The very act of passive resistance can be described as stillness in the midst of turmoil, a willingness to subject the body to the chaos of abuse and social rejection while uniting the ultimate purposes of that resistance to the Holy Spirit. Incredibly, abuse loses its power when it confronts the unified resolve of a community and the personal commitment of its individuals. Throughout the history of segregation in North America and around the world, people of color died at the hands of the dominant culture. The meaning of these deaths seemed to be swallowed by time without affecting the policies of those who assented to the deaths and without awakening those killed and their kin to the power in nonviolent resistance.

When killers kill with the state as a silent partner, when "the killed" see no end to the progressive annihilation of spirit and soul, both succumb to a spiritual disorder. This spiritual disorder is most often characterized by flight—flight from prayer, from intimate relationships, from silence and the potential to hear a divine blessing or rebuke. The only spiritual recompense seems to be that eventually societies that sanction violence against the poor and oppressed inevitably ingest the bile they spew and reap the violence they commit. Further indication of our connection to an embedded divine wisdom arises in our realization that whether we want to or not, we recognize the humanity of other human beings even if our hands are shaping the rope to lynch, even if our fists are formed to strike a spouse.

The question is whether this recognition floats through the consciousness untethered or whether it is deeply rooted in spiritual disciplines that imply the possibility of repentance or redemption. Our postmodern societies seem to have found the balm in consumer practices, noise, sports, video games, and reality shows. But even in the midst of the din, a soul in ecstasy will recognize moves of the spirit.

We Are Marching to Zion, Beautiful, Beautiful Zion

The civil rights marches of the 1960s were contemplative—sometimes silent, sometimes drenched with song, but always contemplative. This may mean within the context of a desperate quest for justice that while weary feet traversed well-worn streets, hearts leaped into the lap of God. While children were escorted into schools by national guardsmen, the song "Jesus Loves Me" became an anthem of faith in the face of contradictory evidence. You cannot face German shepherds and fire hoses with your own resources; there must be God and stillness at the very center of your being. Otherwise, you will spiral into the violence that threatens you. What saves you is the blessed merger of intuitive knowing with rationality, pain, and resolve.

Like a spiritual earthquake, the resolve of the marchers affirmed the faith of foremothers and forefathers. Each step was a reclamation of the hope unborn. Each marcher embodied the communal affirmation of already/not yet sacred spaces. Ronald Grimes describes ritual processionals that bear many of the markers of civil rights marches: "A procession is the linearly ordered, solemn movement of a group through chartered space to a known destination to give witness, bear an esteemed object, perform a rite, fulfill a vow, gain merit, visit a shrine."[1]

Applying Grimes's elements to civil rights marches, I find that the spiritual destination of these justice processions was the consciousness of the nation. The witness was that nonviolence was the most powerful weapon within human control. The esteemed object was the sacred *imago Dei* in dark bodies. The rite was the act of walking in community to challenge the forces of evil and death. The vow was the unspoken commitment to redeem the sacrifices of the ancestors. The shrine was within; the merit was God's favor extended to people of faith and obedience. These contemplative acts moved the community toward the fulfillment of one small aspect of the beloved community: the end of legally sanctioned segregation.

The sacred act of walking together toward justice was usually preceded by a pre-march meeting that began with a prayer service, where preaching, singing, and exhortation prepared the people to move toward the hope they all held. This hope was carefully explicated by the leadership as a fulfillment of God's promises. As a consequence, the movement that spilled from the churches to the streets was a ritual enactment of a communal faith journey toward the *basileia* of God.

Protesters through their silence and songs would amplify their humanity for the world to see. As Grimes notes in his discussion of ritual practices, "processants do not occupy centralized sacred space. Instead, they carry their 'center' with them" as they move toward their destination.[2] Although Grimes presents processions as affirmations of established beliefs, there is the potential for inversion.[3] Grimes appears to see inversion in the presentation of an order and movement that has all of the attributes of a formal processional but either parodies (as in Mardi Gras) or confronts (as in the civil rights movement). For marchers with King, the inversion occurred the moment African Americans entered public space where they had heretofore been deemed invisible. Not only were de jure and de facto prohibitions that separated the races tumbling down during each multiracial procession, but the sudden eruption of Black presence into public space as peaceful contemplative activists shattered the social order's demonically constructed images of indolent Black buffoons and criminals. These suppositions relied upon consistent replication of negative images of Africana people to maintain segregation. The antidote to this ethereal poison was presence, peaceful sacrifice, and unrelenting resolve.

The end result was that a purportedly Christian nation was forced to view its Black citizens as a prototype of the suffering God, absorbing violence into their own bodies without retaliation. By contrast, stalwart defenders of the old order found themselves before God and their own reflective interiority with fire hoses, whips, and ropes in their hands. The crisis created by contemplative justice seeking guaranteed the eventual end of overt practices of domination, for domination could not withstand the steady gaze of the inner eye of thousands of awakened people.

Grimes's theory of ritual provides an interesting lens to view the contemplative practices of the African American community but does not work as well to explicate the struggles of other Africana communities. Grimes contends that when dance and music are added to processions, they become a parade. He argues that "when dancing shifts from circularity and symmetry to linearity and asymmetry, the religious climate is likely to shift from prophetic criticism to priestly conservatism."[4] Although this may be true among certain cultures and religions, it has less credence among people who value music and dance as an opportunity to mediate social conflict or to provide conduits to the transcendent. An excellent example can be found in South Africa. As the young people began to engage the power of the state and its apartheid policies, they would often dance throughout the night in tight circles that would unwind and process. The drums and rhythmic shouts and songs embodied the very essences of defiance and prophetic critique. The key for Grimes seems to be whether the processionists are deemed to be integral to the dominant order. When they are not, they are free within the liminal space of their social isolation to choose their methods of communal expression.

The contemplative locus of the movement should not come as a surprise to those who survived the twentieth century. The crucial spiritual engagements were spun like a luminous web from the worn pews of Black churches, tin shacks in South Africa, and Native American reservations. Shouts, prayers and shut-ins, and ritual enactments of the elders and ancestors prepared the way so that when Harriet Tubman headed into the thickets and Rosa Parks settled into her seat, there was a contemplative faith history ready to accompany their acts of justice seeking and activism.

A New View of Community

The turning point for North America was its acceptance of the moral lynchpin upon which the movement staked its claims. In the stillness that infused the hush arbors and prayer meetings, a vision of justice emerged that could not be legislated. It emanated from divine interiority. Those marching merely reflected this reality. The mark of a Spirit-informed movement is incongruity. The sheer power of the systems of oppression looms impenetrably just before it crumbles in seemingly inexplicable ways. Will prayerful marching around Jericho actually cause the walls to tumble? "Well, maybe," comes the unconvinced reply. These are natural events. If a system is corrupt and corroded from the inside out, then any shaking will cause it to fall. Believers and skeptics find common ground in this assertion. Yet the mark of dominant orders is their expert ability to hide the rot and internal decay so that those who act in opposition find themselves facing the illusion of a behemoth that cannot be defeated.

Who could have predicted that America's apartheid would fall as decisively as the walls of Jericho, when the people marched around the bastions of power carrying little more than their faith and resolve? How audacious it is to take what is given—the remnants of a chattel community, the vague memories of mother Africa, and a desperate need to be free—and translate those wisps into a multi-cultural, multivalent liberative vision of community. The idea of a beloved community emerged from the deeply contemplative activities of a besieged people. My own participation in these activities is crucial to my understanding of civil rights activism as contemplative.

Come Before Winter

New Haven, the city of my upbringing, is a wintry place, a city of demand and debate. Although there are probably colder places, I am always reminded of Paul's entreaty "come before winter." The urgency to get things done in such places is palpable. This town nestled by the sea was the site of Amistad refuge and Panther trials. After relocating here, my family joined a socially activist and upwardly mobile African American Congregational Church. Although the church eventually became affiliated with the United Church of Christ, its most memorable affiliation was with the Underground Railroad, with hiding stations in its basement. In the lower levels of the church, dank and mysterious spaces still held their secrets. As children, we sometimes thought that if you listened hard enough, you could almost hear the sounds of feet "runnin' for free."

This spiritual way station, which sat in the shadows of Yale University and the Winchester gun factory, evoked the danger, irony, and earnestness of a people on the move. Critical elements of faith, justice, and struggle seemed to coalesce in New Haven, Connecticut. Our church participated in the civil rights struggles and, at the same time, tried like crazy to mentor model citizens of a republic that resoundingly and smugly resisted those yearnings.

I grew up in the midst of these complexities. From the church's pews, I went to Selma to march with King and then returned to have my church-affiliated debutante ball. The messages were conflicting: resist and succeed. But how does one resist the systems that must be appeased to allow those successes? The church that nurtured me also confused me. We were being mentored and guided toward a life considered to be Black middle class. Although we did not realize it at the time, this generational class leap would take all of our intellectual and emotional efforts. We would begin a one-way journey toward "integration" by identifying with the dominant culture and mimicking its rituals and lifestyles. Legal barriers fell so quickly that there was no time to authenticate our choices, to anchor them securely to the cultural flagship of Africana faith and practice. During the sprint toward equality, however, certain perspectives surfaced in ways that allowed the community to hold contradictory beliefs and ideas. My debutante ball was a prime example.

Marching for Freedom
Waltzing with Upward Mobility

Although in retrospect it seems painfully incongruous to have a debutante ball in an era of Panther trials, Malcolm X's emergence, and the escalating civil rights movement in the South, this is exactly what we did. But before the curtsy came the march. Soon after the four little girls were killed in the church bombing in Alabama, our church, Dixwell Avenue Congregational in New Haven, Connecticut, prepared to send a group of teens and adults south to participate in the marches. We would go into small towns to support civil rights workers who were risking their lives every day.[1]

After the big march in Selma, we returned to prepare for our "social debut." In many ways, the ball was an inversion ritual that challenged the status quo because African American girls in my community were preparing to bow into a society that considered us to be invisible. We were teens searching for identity amid the blurred events of a nonviolent revolution and practiced curtsies. One thing was certain: our days of invisibility were numbered when we declared our "beingness" in a white dress with a hoop skirt. Long before James Brown sang "I'm Black and I'm Proud," club women and church ushers decided that their children would defy Jim Crow and dance with that old black magic, self-esteem. Faced with daunting personal and communal challenges, we affirmed the *imago Dei* in dark-skinned, broken, gay, and feminine bodies.

The civil rights marches and debutante ball were rites of passage that seemed completely unrelated. I wanted the dots connected for me; instead, we were given experiential puzzle pieces to decipher and situate in our individual and communal lives. Such initiation rites inevitably draw the initiate inward, as this is the only site of potential resolution. And so, after developing contemplative practices on our front porches and on well-worn pews, we marched for freedom and waltzed into a society that rejected us.

Confusion was inevitable. Although there were probably myriad reasons for the confusion, one cause seems evident: the development of an interior life was also associated with assimilation, gentility, and upward mobility. Further confusion resulted because the community that needed us to bring our youth and energy to the enhancement of the common good also encouraged us to make great leaps toward materialistic successes. As pioneers on integration's frontier, we had to trade memories of our days as elementary-school anchorites and social revolutionaries for "cross-over careers" that would catapult us into the "white world." The stillness that had evolved on the porch was translated into career moves and civil practices that would create cataclysmic cultural changes.

Like the iceman who delivered ice to my great-grandmother in the 1930s and '40s, I bear phantom traces of all that has gone before. I have been told stories about the iceman, who would use sharp tongs to pick up a block of ice. If he miscalculated, that piece would bear the marks of the tongs, sharp, deeply carved, and temporary. Grandma Booker would often say that once the ice melted, you could no longer see the marks, but you remembered where they had been. "Life is just like that," she would conclude. Assimilation tactics subliminal and overt are like the tong-scarred ice. The community would be with you whether you wanted it to or not. Its invisible imprint lasted long after your exodus.

Yet even as we prepared to venture into a wider social setting, there was the call to connect to the struggle of the community. Since I had not yet heard of the scientific theory of complementarity—the ability to hold diametrically opposed ideas or realities within the same conceptual microcosm—my friends and I considered material success and social consciousness to be alternatives that would lead in completely divergent directions. Most of us began to move toward the possibility of individual success rather than communal well-being. This was not a rejection of the community but rather a commissioning. We would be explorers in the white world. We would be educated, and then when we had achieved our goals, we would uplift the race.

How could we know that while the civil rights movement was gaining strength, the strengths of the Black community were being dissipated?

During these years of dissolution and overcoming, the Black Church was a safe harbor and a spiritual refuge. In fact, during the years of slavery and oppression it had become a taken-for-granted necessity. Now the yearning within the community was for individual achievement and competitive feats. To enter this race toward equality meant turning away from communal values. It also required that we put aside the ancestral legacies that had sustained us.

Notwithstanding double standards with regard to gender and sexual identity, most were committed across class lines to the wholeness and protection of the entire community. The movement toward diversification of this closed system was inevitable as social constraints eased, but we had no regrets because we believed with all of our hearts that the community would be there if and when we ever returned. We were wrong.

It is not easy to find that locus of spiritual support anymore. It has slipped from view. In just one generation, those who had the means to leave have become economic and cultural exiles. Even those who were left behind are not the same. It is nearly impossible to recognize the historical antecedents to "thug life" and millennialism in the hopes of the community that preceded them. Certainly, the widespread focus on immediate gratification and materialism is confounding for a people who made survival an art form.

Survival as an art form was encoded in transformative ideas about community that far exceeded the dream language that cloaked it. Its contours could be described as a fully clothed prophetic vision that emerged from the yearning of the people. It was such a hopeful time. With the constraints of segregation loosened, those who had faithfully prayed for deliverance believed that the community would emerge as inevitably as an iceberg on the Arctic horizon. We assumed that all goals would be reached in progressive and linear increments. Instead, we were faced with cycles of accomplishment and defeat. Rabbi Arthur Waskow retrospectively recognizes the cycles of oppression that justice-loving people experience: "In every generation there will be a pharaoh that rises to oppress us."[2]

Some of the pharaohs of the twenty-first century are white, some are people of color. The oppressors of communities of color no longer wear white sheets; instead, they are law enforcers and policymakers. No one could have predicted that the same community that marched and sat in together would begin to kill one another for sneakers, territory, and drugs. The new pharaohs arose as internalized task masters in the guise of nihilism and self-hatred. No one could have predicted that the studding of Black males enforced during slavery would be voluntarily assumed by postmodern Black men who now sire but will not father or mothers who bear but will not suckle. No one could have predicted down-low brothers who secretly engage in sporadic high-risk same-sex liaisons while maintaining macho love matches with unsuspecting women, homophobia in the churches, and a deafening ecclesial silence in response to violence and discrimination against the LGBTQIA community.

Some attribute these self-destructive acts to conspiracy, the purposeful targeting of ethnic communities for widespread drug distribution. This is an allegation I can neither confirm nor deny. However, I can ask the question: where is the moral resolve that kept the justice movements on the path toward fruition without money, without resources, with only a community beloved and contemplated? To reclaim we must once again pause and consider the contours of this community. Do we still have the same goals? Do King's words still ring true? Where is the community called beloved when we need it most?

Henri Nouwen describes the essence of community from a spiritual perspective. He says, "the basis of the Christian community is not the family or social or economic equality, or shared oppression or complaint, or mutual attraction . . . but the divine call."[3] This is an important aspect of community that is overlooked. According to Nouwen, the Christian community is a waiting community.[4] But it is also a group of people who pray the reality of their sense of belonging into being.

In recent years, many of us bemoan the failure of the beloved community to materialize in an objective way. It seems to be stuck in a time warp, tangled up in dream language and unrealistic expectations of reconciliation without repentance. False reconciliations expect victims of oppression to forget, absolve, and move on without acknowledgment of misdeeds or repentance, and for oppressors to apologize but keep the spoils of unmerited privilege. This is not the type of reconciliation that King recommended. When King painted a picture of the ultimate goals of the community called beloved, he necessarily—for reasons of time and rhetorical impact—omitted the tedious steps and sacrifices that would pave the way for its emergence.

But the most hidden aspect of community formation was the necessity of intentional contemplative practices as a spiritual precursor to the participation of a co-creating God. Nouwen makes the connection clear. It is through rituals of silence, word, song, and gesture that we indicate our readiness for the indwelling of God. It is through the sacred space that emerges in the Black Church during abiding times, which may or may not be silent, that the contours of community become visible.

Public Mystics
Letting the Light Shine

There are always those who lead by example, who slash through the thick brush to prepare a path, whose prayers are remembered, and whose deeds live long after they have become ancestors. The people that I have selected as contemplatives in this chapter are exemplary. Some are known for their leadership or courage, but few are known for their contemplative contributions. I am seeking the ineffable in the ordinary, the mystical in the mundane, the transcendent in the midst of pragmatic justice-seeking acts. As a consequence, the method of inquiry for this chapter shifts slightly from critical analysis to vignette.

The exemplars come from different eras, but most are from the twentieth century. The reader will recognize the names of Rosa Parks, Howard Thurman, Fannie Lou Hamer, and Martin Luther King Jr. Because much has been written about each of these figures, we think that we know all about them. Yet there are gaps even in the imaginative projections that purport to encapsulate their lives. What does it mean to be a public mystic, a leader whose interiority and communal reference points must intersect? How does one called to such monumental tasks traverse the landscape of public expectations and inner longing? The questions that inform this chapter focus on the nature of contemplation in the lives of well-known civil rights leaders.

FANNIE LOU HAMER:
THE SICK AND TIRED "SAINT"

What manner of woman was this? She had such a familiar face and figure that you expected to see her at your own family reunion. The moment you set eyes on her, you recognized her as a relative even if you knew that she was not. She had the visage of a laboring woman and a determination to match the presence. Although her body was familiar, it was not her own. The system of segregation could kill, beat, or disfigure her at will. The assault upon her humanity was complete when she was subjected to one of the first involuntary hysterectomies (also known as a "Mississippi appendectomy") inflicted on poor rural women in the South.[1]

She was born on October 6, 1917, in the violent and oppressive county of Montgomery, Mississippi, and grew up in a loving but poverty-stricken sharecropping family. Rosetta Ross, in her excellent account of Black women in the civil rights movement, quotes Hamer on the issue of work in Mississippi: "We worked all the time . . . just worked and then we would be hungry and my mother was clearing up a new ground trying to help feed us for $1.25 a day. She was using an axe, just like a man."[2] While wielding the axe, Hamer's mother lost an eye. It seems that one hardship followed upon another, and Hamer and her family were trapped in a system of indentured labor.

I have chosen her as a contemplative exemplar because of her spiritual focus and resolve. Her practices spoke to the depth of her contemplative spirit. In the face of catastrophic suffering, Hamer worked, loved, sang, and resisted the powers that be. She was jailed, beaten, and hunted by the enforcers of the social order after registering to vote. The treatment was so brutal that Andrew Young was sent to get her out of jail. Yet she was kind to jailers who had been beating her for a week.[3] Where do you go in your spirit and mind when someone is beating you mercilessly? What peace have you summoned to smile at the abuser?

I remember Fannie Lou Hamer as a figure of the civil rights movement whose tenacity brought the Democratic Party to a temporary accountability and struck fear into the Republicans. All of this was not-so-distant history until I met one of her colleagues at a conference convened by Charles Marsh that focused on lived theology and civil courage. It was a unique gathering of academics and elders of the movement, her friends and confidantes, and warriors of the Mississippi race wars.

For some reason still unknown to me, I could not pay attention to the plenary address given by Victoria Gray Adams. She was a regal woman, a friend of Hamer, and an activist in her own right. Her address began carefully. Her speech was measured; the cadence was slow. She had lived so many decades in a struggle for respectability that now, in front of these serious religious scholars, she was determined not to stumble or misspeak. Unfortunately, her careful speech lulled me into a reverie. I would like to say that I entered a contemplative space, but I think that I fell asleep. I deeply regretted this lapse. How often do you get to hear Fannie Lou Hamer's contemporary speak about her life and the movement to which all of us had dedicated our lives?

In the evening, when the stress of the day was over, I sat with Adams's husband as he talked of hurried clandestine meetings, fear, and courage in the face of insurmountable odds. He mentioned the calm that always preceded the storm and the sense of destiny that did not need words to empower it. They were in this together, come what may. When Adams joined us, I asked my stupid question: "Why did Fannie Lou Hamer die so young?" The answer seems obvious to those who know that Hamer died from the ravages of diabetes, cancer, hypertension, and the lack of medical care in the richest country in the world. Adams looked at me with a mix of weariness and patience. "Don't you get it?" she said. "If it hadn't been for the civil rights movement she would have died sooner." No, I didn't get it. So I persisted: "She had serious medical conditions, but what does that have to do with the movement?" The griot emerged in Mrs. Adams as she settled herself down on a bench in the fancy museum where the gathering was being held. She placed her hand over mine and said, "She picked cotton. Do you know what that means?" She was kind; she did not even wince at the naïveté of this dislocated Yankee. Instead, she continued: "She was worn out from heat, and cotton, and

trying to raise her children in a black-child-killin'
place."[4]

It had never occurred to me that the civil rights
movement could become a monastic space, an
opportunity for respite for a woman who had been
"buked and scorned" by the Black-woman/man/
child-killing system of the day. Even in her beatings
there was peace because at least the forces of evil were
being dragged into the light of day with every blow.
I realize that there may be abused persons who will
misinterpret my meaning. Options and responses
to abuse differ from situation to situation; however,
there is never a time when I would lift up submission
to abuse as a model response. Nevertheless, when the
system wields its life-crushing power, counterintui-
tive responses often yield the most fruitful results.
Hamer was centered; she drew power from the example of her parents in their struggle to transcend the
impossible situation of their lives. She faced daunting odds, as she was not dealing with an abusive
individual but instead the power of federal, state,
and local governments and cultural traditions that
deemed her to be a nonperson. This designation of
nonpersonhood did not deter her, for her contemplative entry into a deeper "knowing" came through her
commitment to nonviolence. Adherence to the spiritual disciplines of civil rights activism required that

she love the crucifier, bless the torturer, embrace the jailer, and pray for his or her salvation. She did this and more. This description of Hamer's piety and commitment brings me to a stopping point. I am not one who relishes the glorification of good deeds in the lives of individuals. I shy away from the reporting of laudatory exploits because as an ethicist I believe that goodness is our ordinary task, that it is the sinew between soul and spirit strengthened by the choice to do what is fitting and right. Yet the example that Hamer sets requires recognition.

According to her friend Virginia Gray Adams, "her back hurt and her spirit waged war without proper food or medicine. So when the movement came, there was rest"—not the rest that pervades the lives of most contemplatives, but rest nonetheless. Rest as you tell Congress to let your people go. Rest as you testify and lead a delegation off the floor of the Democratic Convention. Rest comes as rest comes—sometimes in the great feather beds of the wealthy and sometimes just a step away from hard labor. When it comes, it is balm to the spirit and solace to the soul. This is a rest that wafts from a wellspring of intentional justice seeking as spiritual practice. These practices allow one to live in and out of the body and to inhabit hope as an ethereal but more permanent enfleshment. Fannie Lou Hamer was cloistered in an activist movement, finding her focus, restoration, and life in God in the midst of the beloved community already here and yet coming.

And so on April 14, 1977, the plain-talking, hard-working saint from Mississippi, an unlikely prophet who was "sick and tired of being sick and tired," died at the age of fifty-nine. In his eulogy Andrew Young said, "She literally, along with many of you, shook the foundations of this nation. . . . Mrs. Hamer was special, but she was also representative. Hundreds of women spoke up and . . . learned the lessons that inspired the women's movement."[5] The story ends here, but it is the beginning of stories that will be told wherever justice-loving people gather. Once upon a time there was a contemplative mother, a brave and wise woman of few words who entered the civil rights movement as a novitiate enters a convent—not for retreat but for the restorative love of the community and the space to fight for justice. She spoke when speaking was necessary and led always by example, letting her little light shine.

MARTIN LUTHER KING JR.: RIDING A SPIRITUAL TIDAL WAVE

A positive religious faith does not offer an illusion that we shall be exempt from pain and suffering, nor does it imbue us with the idea that life is a drama of unalloyed comfort and untroubled ease. Rather, it instills us with the inner equilibrium needed to face strains, burdens, and fears that inevitably come and assures us that the universe is trustworthy and God is concerned.[6]

So much has been written about King, and yet it seems that he becomes more and more opaque as time goes on. This may be because we project upon this great spiritual leader our retrospective critiques and expectations. I think of King as a great contemplative, one who used the spiritual essence of nonviolence as a tool for liberating the social order and the spiritual authority of a denigrated people. The power of the contemplative life becomes evident as we watch a man steeped in the hierarchical and rather static and entrenched ecclesial systems of denominational church life change direction. King's intention when he returned to the South was to take his comfortable and prepared place in that long line of preachers in his family; however, it was not to be.

As events unfolded, it often seemed that King was running behind the movement, representing it, speaking on its behalf, but allowing its life to come from the people who were putting their lives on the line. Truth be told, it was not the Black Church in its static and familiar denominational guise, but the meta-actual church embodied in the resolve of young people that caught and cast the vision for the visionary.

The institutional Black Church did not understand what was going on until the movement was well underway. As Jesse Jackson notes, it is only in retrospect that the Black Church has fully embraced King and a revisionist version of his life and beliefs.[7] They are still not comfortable with the King who rejected capitalism and used antiwar rhetoric. King is blurred and co-opted in our postmodern era because we have assigned him to a static identity and ironed out the contradictions that are often found in the lives of contemplatives.

The specific characteristics that point to the contemplative aspects of King's life include authenticity that did not emanate from inherited respectability, spiritual transience that allowed him to follow the impetus of the communal and divine will rather than imposing a direction, and awareness of the rhythms of deliverance, coming in and out of exile. Speaking with an authentic voice in an age of formal oration is not easy. King was a preacher, but his public voice exceeded the boundaries of homiletical prowess. Instead, he used his voice to amplify the voices of the voiceless. When you hear him or read his speeches, you hear not only the rhythms of Black

Baptist oratory and the utterances of a living prophet but also the voice of the community. He spoke as a human megaphone, articulating commonly held beliefs as if the community spoke in unison through him. His words echoed in all hearts, even in those of his opponents.

Spiritual transience is the story of biblical call. Inevitably you find yourself in places you never expected to be. The willingness to wander at the bidding of the Spirit is settled long before the journeys begin. It is settled during prayer and contemplation when desires and self-direction give way in favor of spiritual leading. King found himself in situations that reason would not choose, witnessing where politically astute leaders would fear to tread. Before racism was dead, his talk turned to the necessity of an antiwar stance; before the South had relented, he was demonstrating in the North and facing the intractable systems of those who hide their racial disdain behind their liberal acts. He seemed to be following and listening, adjusting for the moment-by-moment changes that occurred as he journeyed with a community on the move.

Finally, King recognized the rhythms that prevail when you are coming in and out of exile. There are no linear paths when you follow the contemplative way. Escaping one set of circumstances usually invites another set. If you are coming out of Egypt, you are going into the wilderness; emerging from segregation, you enter the exilic event of legally imposed integration. In the realm of the Spirit, stationary goals are mythologies that obscure intersecting realities. The signposts that mark progress are internal as well as external. The indicator of King's purposes and progress came from his implementation of agape love.

King defined *agape* as "the love of God operating in the human heart."[8] The journey toward complete dependence on God culminated with his famous "I See the Promised Land" speech. The metaphorical language that King used hints at an inward journey. Surrounded by threatening situations, he had prayed through and had seen with his spiritual eye both the promised land and the coming of the Lord. Like Moses, he had seen but would not inhabit. The reasons are God's.

The parallel to Moses seems obvious, but there are also spiritual intersections with the prophet Anna. She was allowed to see Jesus before she died. Although she would not be around for the sermons, miracles, or acts of deliverance, her sight was sufficient—sufficient because she saw not just with natural eyes but also with the spiritual and contemplative depth that allows God's Spirit to respond to the pleas of the heart. On the night before King's death, we all saw the face of a man who had been in the presence of the holy and who feared nothing. As a consequence, the shot that fulfilled his prophecy was horrendous but also anticlimactic.

King had just the night before reassured us that the person or motive responsible for dispatching his human body was of little concern. King had already relinquished his life to God on the mountaintop. But where was that mountain? At the time of this writing, I lived in Memphis, a city that had not forgiven itself for being the site of King's death. I can tell you that there are no mountains in Memphis, a few hills, but no crests of rock that touch the clouds. So King's spiritual mountaintop is a very interesting metaphoric choice.

I believe that his use of this phrase was a hint about his own contemplative journey. Perhaps the steepest climb on the life journey is toward death. It requires trust that may not have developed during life; it requires relinquishment of attachments. It is an arduous task. When Jesus sweats in Gethsemane, he is also mountain climbing, relinquishing, and accepting. At the top of this mountain of obedience and necessity, King communed with God and was offered freedom in ways that he had never imagined.

During this theophany, God's intent was revealed to him like a film preview, giving King the impetus to say, "I've looked over. And I've seen the Promised Land. I may not get there with you. But I want you to know tonight, that we as a people will get to the Promised Land. And I'm happy tonight. I'm not worried about anything. I'm not fearing any man. Mine eyes have seen the glory of the coming of the Lord."[9] King's contemplative turn toward the source of all being gave him peace. He was at the right place during the right time in history, when God's deliverance rolled down like water through the bastions of injustice.

ROSA PARKS: CONTEMPLATION AND LAY ACTIVISM

I had no idea that history was being made. I was just tired of giving in. Somehow, I felt that what I did was right by standing up to that bus driver. I did not think about the consequences. I knew that I could have been lynched, manhandled, or beaten when the police came. I chose not to move. When I made that decision, I knew that I had the strength of the ancestors with me.[10]

Any anchorite worth her salt seals herself up in a church and dedicates her life to the worship of God, but a bus, a cell on wheels—can this really be a space of respite and revolution? In the tradition of those who sacrifice with prayer and dedication, Rosa Parks prepared herself spiritually and practically for the tasks to come. Her ten days at Highlander Folk School began the healing process within.[11] She noted that during her brief stay she interacted with whites as equals and extinguished some of the anger and resentment she had internalized.

Some say that she was a "professional" resister because of her training at the Highlander School—maybe, maybe not. Battered self-respect and weary feet are equally sound motivations for refusing to leave a bus seat when challenged. But this is all in retrospect. At the time of her resistance nothing was certain. The news story very well could have been: "A middle-aged black woman was killed in a bus incident today after her refusal to obey the laws of segregation." At the moment that you stare into the fires stoked by oppression, seven times their usual heat, you cannot know that one "like the son of God" will be with you—all you can see is fire. Yet she sat. While people yelled at her and the police threatened, she sat. The stillness within became a sign of external dignity and a model of contemplative activism.

When she was asked to vacate her seat, three other Black passengers were also asked to move from a row of seats behind the whites-only section. They obeyed; she did not. As a lay woman acquainted with the struggle for justice, her actions become the quintessential expression of the power of the people.

What could be more contemplative then the act of sitting silently? No matter that Parks spent ten days at Highlander. No matter that her middle-class upbringing was necessary to forestall the moral criticism used as a cover to indict protesters. In silence, in peace she sat.

Parks sparked a movement because she could be trusted. Who knew where the leaders were getting their power? They were in the position to broker deals, to negotiate with both sides of an issue, and even to be compensated for taking a particular stance in volatile community situations. Through this lay woman, a community of Africans in the Americas heard the drumbeat of inevitability and sat down all over the South. At lunch counters and segregated church services they sat. They were not all in one place, but they sat together as the blows of the institutions of segregation rained on their heads.

"At the jailhouse, Parks asked if she could have a drink from the water fountain and was told it was for whites only. She then was fingerprinted, booked, and put in a cell with two other black women, one of whom gave her a drink of water from a dark metal mug."[12] Cool waters that refresh the soul can come from waters in a dark metal mug. Who would not prefer a spring or fresh-flowing river? But when those sources have been co-opted or removed from your reach, water from a mug in a friend's hand is a blessed offering. Once in a generation there is a Thérèse of Lisieux, a Sojourner Truth, a Fannie Lou Hamer whose refusal to succumb becomes the center of the movement toward justice. Like Queen Esther, Rosa Parks emerges at such a time as this to embody not just nonviolence but also the contemplative strength of the people expressed through individual and community action.

SUE BAILEY AND HOWARD THURMAN: LISTEN FOR THE SOUND OF THE GENUINE WITHIN

The Thurmans are trailblazers in the arena of contemplative and mystical studies. Because much has been written about their lives, this vignette seeks only insight into their public mysticism. Although there were many exemplars with spiritual depth in Africana traditions, few claimed those gifts as the center of their religious thought. Howard Thurman did just that. Biographers imply that he had spiritual inclinations from the beginning, having been born "with the veil" in segregated Daytona, Florida. In the Black folk tradition, children born with the veil have second sight and can interpret and connect to the spirit realm. All types of remedies for this "condition" were available. In Howard's case, his ears were pierced to "dissipate clairvoyance."

As far as Howard Thurman is concerned, deep spirituality is not just the result of birthright and folk interpretations; he is also highly cognizant of his place in a broader universe. In *With Head and Heart*, Howard recalls seeing Halley's Comet and feeling connected to something more profound than the petty social arrangements that relegated him to the margins of society.[13] But public mysticism was an unusual choice for Black people in Howard's day. It seemed to be a most impractical pursuit. People wanted normalcy, safety, and opportunity. They heard the elders talk of mystery but relegated those discussions to the private realm. Yet Howard Thurman could not conceive of life without the mystical. His creativity allowed him to translate his sense of centeredness into artful worship services that celebrated ritual and drama.

In 1935 he and his wife, Sue Bailey Thurman, went to India, Burma, and Ceylon. During this trip, they met Mohandas Gandhi and talked with him about the issues of persecution. Sue Bailey was a fascinating woman.[14] Along with her work with Howard in the development of the first interracial, nondenominational church in the United States, she was also an activist who worked tirelessly for women's causes and for the ultimate equal rights of all. Richard Newman describes their work as pilgrimage from the clear-cut context of the Black Church to an unknowing reunion with humankind and the divine.

Walter Fluker, a Howard Thurman scholar and one who knew him and worked with him, discusses a moment of angst in 1980 when he asked Howard for career advice: "Thurman wrote back, 'You must wait and listen for the sound of the genuine that is within. When you hear it, it will be your voice and that will be the voice of God.'"[15] Thurman's recognition that there is no separateness of person, space, or religious inclination is his particular contemplative gift. Thurman reaches beyond the familiar to embrace the possible:

> There is a spirit abroad in life of which the Judaeo-Christian ethic is but one expression. It is a spirit that makes for wholeness and for community. . . . It broods over the demonstrators for justice and brings comfort to the desolate and forgotten who have no memory of what it is to feel the rhythm of belonging. . . . It knows no country and its allies are

to be found wherever the heart is kind and the collective will and the private endeavor seek to make justice where injustice abounds.[16]

Howard and Sue Bailey understood the needs of besieged Africana communities, but they also realized that when you "center down" you may be called to exceed the boundaries of your own community and its needs to embrace your neighbors. Their spiritual witness is that God "so loves the world" with all of its variant faith expressions and that God's Spirit broods over us and sustains us without regard to national or religious boundaries—requiring of us not liturgical conformity but justice, peace, and kind hearts.

MALCOLM X (EL HAJJ MALIK EL SHABAZZ)

Like Augustine, Malcolm X was a contemplative whose life was layered and enriched by multiple conversion experiences. He was born Malcolm Little in 1925. When he died, he was known as El Hajj Malik El Shabazz and better known as Malcolm X. His life was deeply affected by racism and violence at an early age. When he was a young boy, his father, a Baptist preacher and organizer with Marcus

Garvey's Back to Africa movement, was murdered by white dissidents. Malcolm noted that his mother had a premonition of the murder and tried to call her husband back to the house as he headed for town.[17] Malcolm claimed to have the same empathic ability.

The death of his father changed their financial circumstances drastically and precipitated their move north to stay with relatives. There Malcolm drifted into criminal behavior. His autobiography describes the onslaughts of a racist society and his increasingly resistant response to it. He was arrested in 1946 and served a seven-year sentence. It was during his prison term that Malcolm's first conversion experience occurred, and he became aware of the contemplative aspects of his spiritual life. bell hooks offers a unique glimpse of the contemplative Malcolm in confinement:

> Confinement in prison provides the space where Malcolm can engage in uninterrupted critical reflection on his life, where he can contemplate the meaning and significance of human existence. During this period of confinement, he comes face to face with the emptiness of his life, the nihilism. This time for him is akin to "a dark night of the soul." . . . He is overwhelmed with longing, without knowing for what he longs. It is in that space of need that he is offered Islam.[18]

He accepted this lifeline and became deeply committed to the Nation of Islam. His devotion to Elijah Muhammad and his years of celibacy prior to his marriage to Betty Shabazz were elements of his deeply contemplative inclinations. Of this aspect of his life bell hooks says, "Taking a vow of celibacy was one of the ways Malcolm expressed this devotion. He sought no personal love relationships because he felt they would interfere with his spiritual quest, with his commitment to serve his master."[19]

In Malcolm's life, contemplative practices are linked to Islam. Michael Eric Dyson notes the differences between Malcolm's spirituality and the spirituality of the Black Church in his discussion of Spike Lee's 1992 film about Malcolm's life. Dyson says:

> The markers of black spirituality have been dominated by the Christian cosmos; the themes, images, and ideas of black spiritual life are usually evoked by gospel choirs enthralled in joyous praise or a passionate preacher engaged in ecstatic proclamation. Never before in American cinema has an alternative black spirituality been so intelligently presented.[20]

Malcolm evidenced a quiet authority that drew its strength from the rhetoric of political empowerment and a focused spiritual intent. Malcolm's devotion to Elijah Muhammad was contingent upon the integrity of Elijah's leadership. His moral intensity was not based on ethical formulas or rules; rather, it emanated from a deeply resonant inner reality. As Elijah Muhammad's moral failures became apparent and Malcolm's public power soared, the relationship ended, and Malcolm had another conversion experience.

When I use the word *conversion*, I am not implying any judgment as to the veracity or context for these shifts of religious orientation. Some scholars problematize the "convenience" of his last conversion. I do not think it matters; what is more important is Malcolm's willingness to journey, even when the path requires a rejection of values once held dearly. And so Malcolm embraces classical Islamic teachings and journeys to Mecca. During this entire period, his life is punctuated with passionate oratory, critical thinking, and social confrontations. Yet he is grounded in a contemplative tradition that expects a practical translation of the spiritual into accessible resources for the community.

Like King, Malcolm is bigger than life and subject to our romanticized suppositions. Yet his contemplative spirit is a call to the Africana community to recognize the sources of their own oppression, including their complicity in its perpetuation. He often used the language of waking up the "Negro," waking up the nation; decades later, his language has been translated into a rallying cry for the Black Lives Matter movement: Stay Woke. Although Malcolm disavowed his "white devil" language for the language of spiritual unity after Mecca, it is clear that his priority was the uplifting of the Black community. Contemplation did not draw him away from the community. Instead, he became a lightning rod in its midst, impassively drawing the wrath of the dominant culture and those who desperately wanted to assimilate. In his final years, he proposed a dramatic shift from civil to human rights. This is a movement that we are still trying to bring to fruition.

Some followers believe that it was his connection to the wider Islamic and African nations and his attestation that North American Blacks should seek help from and reconnect with the global community that set the assassination in motion. Malcolm knew as he entered the Aurora ballroom that the Nation of Islam did not have the power or reach to affect him in the ways that he was being affected in the last months of his life. In a flash of mystical insight, he called his wife and had her dress and bring his four children to hear his last speech.

Almost fifty years later the mysteries abound. None of the currently living generations will be alive when the truth about the era of assassinations is finally told. Suffice it to say that Malcolm was killed when he broadened the liberation movement to mainstream Islam and the African nations, and Martin was killed when he broadened the civil rights movement from lunch counter sit-ins to a cross-cultural economic battle for the rights of the poor regardless of color.

Malcolm was a wide-eyed mystic—a man who had visions, embraced celibacy, then married without fanfare. Although some scholars accuse him of manipulation in his successive conversions, particularly the final shift to Islam, I wonder if he had simply learned to embrace the faith that embraced him. When the object of your devotion is lost, when the goals that you thought were God-given fail, you have a choice to remain where you are, despondent and bereft, or you may follow the dimly lit path toward greater wisdom. Malcolm and Martin always chose the latter option.

Once-In-A-Lifetime Blooms

According to a romantic myth, the century plant, also known as the Mexican Tree of Life and Abundance or *agave deserti*, blooms only once in its lifetime. In fact, botanists say that it blooms every twenty to thirty years, but once it blooms, it dies. It uses all of its energy to produce the sprouts for the next generation. The civil rights generation is quickly moving toward the history books and the realm of ancestors. Those of us who have lived during this era have shared a unique opportunity to witness the flowering of this rare bloom, the quest for liberation in nonviolent and contemplative ways. Like this "tree of life," which provides food, fodder, twine, soap, and roofing, we have only begun to claim the treasures of a century of activism and contemplative justice seeking.

The contemplatives who led the movements differed significantly in their spiritual orientations, but each journeyed inward and then returned to the community to share the gifts of the spirit. The seeds for the continuance of the liberation movements were produced at great cost. We have an obligation to continue the struggle, but perhaps we are still too close to the movements to find our way to the next site of God's in-breaking justice. Perhaps the next location for change and restoration will be in the hearts of the willing.

Notes

AIN'T GONNA LET NOBODY TURN US AROUND

1 Victor Turner, *The Ritual Process: Structure and Anti-Structure* (Chicago: Aldine, 1969).

IDENTIFYING THE POWER SOURCE

1 James A. Noel, "Contemplation and Social Action in Afro-American Spirituality," *Pacific Theological Review* 22, no. 1 (Fall 1988): 25.
2 Noel, "Contemplation and Social Action in Afro-American Spirituality."
3 Simone Weil, *The Simone Weil Reader*, ed. George A. Panichas (New York: McKay, 1977), 457.

WE ARE MARCHING TO ZION, BEAUTIFUL, BEAUTIFUL ZION

1 Ronald L. Grimes, *Reading, Writing, and Ritualizing: Ritual in Fictive Liturgical and Public Places* (Washington, DC: Pastoral, 1993), 63.
2 Grimes, *Reading, Writing, and Ritualizing*, 64.

3 Grimes, *Reading, Writing, and Ritualizing*, 66.
4 Grimes, *Reading, Writing, and Ritualizing*, 65.

MARCHING FOR FREEDOM

1 I have fully documented the details of my experience in Selma in Barbara A. Holmes, *Race and the Cosmos: An Invitation to View the World Differently* (Harrisburg, PA: Trinity Press, 2002).
2 Rabbi Arthur Waskow, Shalom Institute, Fortieth Anniversary of the March on Washington, C-SPAN, August 23, 2003.
3 Henri J. M. Nouwen, *Reaching Out: The Three Movements of the Spiritual Life* (New York: Doubleday, 1986), 153.
4 Nouwen, *Reaching Out*.

PUBLIC MYSTICS

1 Flora Wilson Bridges, *Resurrection Song: African-American Spirituality* (Maryknoll, NY: Orbis, 2001), 100, quoting Kay Mills, *This Little Light of Mine: The Life of Fannie Lou Hamer* (New York: Dutton, 1993), 17.
2 Rosetta E. Ross, *Witnessing and Testifying: Black Women, Religion, and Civil Rights* (Minneapolis: Fortress Press, 2003), 93.
3 Bridges, *Resurrection Song*, 102.
4 Conversation with Virginia Gray Adams, Lived Theology and Civil Courage Conference, Charlottesville, VA, June 12–14, 2002.
5 Remarks of Andrew Young at the funeral of Fannie Lou Hamer, quoted in Lynne Olson, *Freedom's Daughters: The Unsung Heroines of the Civil Rights Movement from 1830 to 1970* (New York: Scribner, 2001), 394.

6   Martin Luther King Jr., *The Strength to Love* (New York: Harper & Row, 1963), excerpted in *A Testament of Hope: The Essential Writings and Speeches of Martin Luther King, Jr.*, ed. James M. Washington (San Francisco: HarperSanFrancisco, 1991), 515.

7   Frank A. Thomas, "Renewing Your Yes," sermon given at Mississippi Boulevard Church, Palm Sunday, April 4, 2004.

8   King, "An Experiment in Love," in *A Testament of Hope*, 19.

9   King, "I See the Promised Land," in *A Testament of Hope*, 286.

10 Rosa Parks with Gregory J. Reed, *Quiet Strength: The Faith, the Hope and the Heart of a Woman Who Changed a Nation* (Grand Rapids, MI: Zondervan, 1994), 23–24.

11 The Highlander Folk School (now Highlander Center) was founded in 1932 by Myles Horton as a grassroots education institution. Many activists in the civil rights movement attended leadership training and other workshops there.

12 Olson, *Freedom's Daughters*, 109.

13 Howard Thurman, *With Head and Heart: The Autobiography of Howard Thurman* (New York: Harcourt Brace Jovanovich, 1979), 265.

14 Sue Bailey Thurman married Howard Thurman on June 12, 1932, two years after the death of his first wife, Kate. Sue was born on August 3, 1903, and attended a school in Washington, DC, run by Nannie Helen Burroughs. She was also educated at the Lucretia Mott School, Spelman Seminary, and finally Oberlin College. When she met Howard, she was a music instructor at Hampton Institute. She was the founding editor of the *Aframerican Woman's Journal*, which was the official journal of the National Council of Negro Women. In 1952, she

published *Pioneers of Negro Origin in California.* She died on Christmas Day in 1996 at the age of ninety-three.

15 Michele N-K Collison, "Resurrecting the Thurman Legacy for the Next Millennium," *Black Issues in Higher Education*, November 11, 1999, 25.

16 Howard Thurman, *The Luminous Darkness* (New York: Harper & Row, 1965), 22–23.

17 Alex Haley, *The Autobiography of Malcolm X* (New York: Grove, 1965), 9.

18 bell hooks, *Yearning: Race, Gender, and Cultural Politics* (Boston: South End, 1990), 80.

19 hooks, *Yearning,* 83.

20 Michael Eric Dyson, *Making Malcolm: The Myth and Meaning of Malcolm X* (New York: Oxford University Press, 1995), 141.

Suggested Reading

Alexander, Michelle. *The New Jim Crow: Mass Incarceration in the Age of Colorblindness*. New York: New Press, 2010.

Baldwin, James. *The Fire Next Time*. New York: Dell Book, 1962.

Baldwin, Lewis V. *Never Leave Us Alone: The Prayer Life of Martin Luther King Jr.* Minneapolis: Fortress Press, 2010.

Cannon, Katie G. *Katie's Canon: Womanism and the Soul of the Black Community*. New York: Continuum, 1995.

Cone, James H. *The Cross and the Lynching Tree*. Maryknoll, NY: Orbis, 2011.

———. *God of the Oppressed*. New York: Seabury, 1975.

Perkinson, James W. *White Theology: Outing Supremacy in Modernity*. New York: Palgrave Macmillan, 2004.